·IRISH·
BLESSINGS

Irish Prayers and Blessings for all occasions

PAT FAIRON

◆

ILLUSTRATED BY JOANNA MARTIN

Chronicle Books

First published in 1992 by
The Appletree Press Ltd, 7 James Street South,
Belfast BT2 8DL
Copyright © 1992, The Appletree Press. Ltd.
Printed in the E.C. All rights reserved.

IRISH BLESSINGS

First published in the United States in 1993 by
Chronicle Books,
275 Fifth Street, San Franscisco,
California 94103

ISBN 0-8118-0342-2

10 9 8 7 6 5 4 3 2 1

Acknowledgements

For my father and mother.
With grateful thanks to Dharmuid O Laoghaire for
permission to draw my choice of prayers and blessings
from his book *Ar b Paidreacha Duchais* where most of
these prayers and blessings are to be found in their
original language – Gaelic. My thanks also to
Padraig O hAdmaill for ensuring that so little was lost
in their translation. Thanks also to Gill and
Macmillan, Dublin, for permission to reproduce some
prayers from Douglas Hyde's *Religious
Songs of Connacht, 1906.*

Introduction

This little collection of prayers and blessings is drawn from the oral traditions of a people who saw God's handiwork in everything about them. Livelihood and life itself was seen as being dependent on God's will. It was only natural, therefore, to ask for His divine help in every aspect of daily life. This impulse is the origin of these simple and beautiful little prayers and blessings.

Pat Fairon
Loughgall, County Armagh
1992

For Father and Mother

For my mother who raised me at her breast
And for my father who raised me
by the work of his bones;
I trust in the Son of God when
they enter his presence
That there will be a hundred thousand
welcomes for them
In the heavens of peace.

On Awakening

May God and the Virgin Mary, who have brought myself and my children from the sleep of death last night to the brightness of today, bring us safe from all danger and deliver us from the enemy of both body and soul.

On Hearing the Cock Crow

"May the light of the sun shine
on us today" say we,
"The son of the virgin is safe"
says the cock,
"Rise up, woman of the house
and get the fire going".

On Seeing the Sun

O God who created the sun, You are the sun
of my soul and I adore Your brightness.
I love You, O Everlasting Light. May I see
You in the bright light of Your glory.

. . .

O king of brightness and the sun
Who knows our worth,
Be with us every day,
Be with us every night,
Be with us every night and day,
Be with us every day and night.

Lighting the Fire

I will light my fire today
In the presence of the holy, heavenly angels,
In the presence of Gabriel
Most beautiful of form,
In the presence of Urial of all beauty,
Without hatred, without envy, without jealousy,
Without fear, without dread of
Anything under the sun,
And with the Holy Son of God as my refuge.
Lord, kindle in my innermost heart
The ember of love
For My enemies, for my relatives,
for my friends,
For the wise, for the foolish, for the wretched.

DIA DUIT

DIA'S MUIRE DUIT

A Greeting

Greeting: God greet you.

Reply: God and Mary greet you

or

God, Mary and Patrick greet you

.   .   .

In Gaelic

Greeting: Dia duit

Reply: Dia's Muire duit

Going Out and About

The belt of Christ about me on my going out
and on my coming in

· · ·

In the name of God who made a pathway of
the waves,
May He bring us safely home at the end of
the day.

· · ·

God be on your road every way you go.

Before Work

May God bless the work.

·   ·   ·

Let's begin in the name of God.

Ending Work

The blessings of God on the souls of the dead,
And may the great God grant us life and health,
And may he prosper our work and
the work of Christians.

Making Bread

The grace of God and the favour of Patrick
on all that I see and all that I do.
The blessing that God put on the five loaves
and two fishes, may He put on this food.

Prayer on Milking a Cow

The blessings of Mary and the blessing of God,
The blessing of the Sun
And the Moon in her road
Of the man in the East and the
Man in the West,
And my blessings be with thee
And be thou blest.

Charm against Backache

May Peter take it and take it Paul,
May Michael take it and take it John,
May Moleesha take it, may Mweelin take
This pain from my back, this savage ache.

Blessing the Cow

The blessing of God on you, cow,
And twice as many blessings on your calf.
Come, Mary, and sit,
Come, Brigid, and milk,
Come, Holy Michael Archangel
And bless the beef,
In the name of the Father, Son
and Holy Spirit.

A Mother's Blessing on a Son
or Daughter Leaving Home

The great God between
Your two shoulder blades
To protect you in your going and returning,
The Son of the Virgin Mary
Be close to your heart,
And the perfect Holy Spirit
Be keeping an eye on you.

Going to Sea or Crossing a River

Going over the deep place,
O God of patience, take them by the hand
In case of a blow from a strong wave.
O Mary, look out for them
And don't leave them.

Grace before Meals

Bless us, O Lord,
Bless our food and drink,
You Who has so dearly redeemed us
And has saved us from evil,
As You have given us this share of food,
May You give us our share of the everlasting
glory.

Grace after Meals

Praise to the King of Plenty,
Praise every time to God,
A hundred praises and thanks to Jesus Christ,
For what we have eaten and shall eat.

Drinking a Health

We will drink this drink
As Patrick would drink it,
Full of grace and spilling over,
Without fighting or quarrelling or hint of shame,
Or knowing that we will last until tomorrow.
We ask the help of our Mother Mary,
For she is our support at all times,
This is our toast to all here present
And may the Son of Grace be helping us.

Going through a Graveyard

God greet you, all gathered here,
  May God and Mary greet you.
As we are now so once were you,
  As you are now so shall we be.
  May all of us prosper under
  The bright King of the world.

Taking Snuff at a Wake

Seven fills of Patrick's Island,
Seven fills of the tomb of Christ,
Of the blessings of the good God
on your soul,
And on the souls of the seven generations
before you.

Three Folds in my Garment

Three folds in my garment
Yet only one garment I bear
Three joints in a finger
Yet only one finger is there
Three leaves in a shamrock
Yet only one shamrock I wear
Frost, ice and snow
Yet these three are nothing but water
Three persons in God
Yet only one God is there

Prayers for the Dead

God be good to their souls
God rest them
God rest their souls
God have mercy on them.

Putting a Child to Sleep

May God bless you, child.
I put you under the protection of Mary
and her Son,
Under the care of Brigid and her cloak,
And under the shelter of God tonight.

Banking the Fire

I preserve this fire as Christ has
preserved everyone.
Mary on the roof ridge, Brigid in the middle,
And the eight most powerful angels
in the City of Grace
Protect this house and this hearth
and safeguard its people.

· · ·

Let us bank this fire in honour
of Holy Patrick.
May our house not be burnt or
our people murdered,
And may the bright sun of tomorrow shine
on us all, at home or abroad.

I Make this Bed Tonight

In the name of the Father, the Son
and the Holy Spirit,
In the name of the night we were begot,
In the name of the day we were baptised,
In the name of each and every saint and apostle
That is in Heaven

For a Happy Death

When your eyes shall be closing
And your mouth be opening
And your senses be slipping away.
When your heart shall grow cold
And your limbs be old
God comfort your soul that day.

Lighting the Light

Saviour, may You give heavenly light to every
poor soul that has left this world and to every
poor soul we wish to pray for.

Putting Out the Light

May God not put out the light of Heaven on
our soul or on the souls of the dead who are
gone before us with the sign of faith.

On Seeing the New Moon

On this saint's day which has brought in this new moon, as we are in good health at its coming, may we be in good health when it goes and when it comes again.

(Said standing when one sees the new moon)

On Lying Down

I lie down with my dear God,
May my dear God lie with me,
The two hands of God about my waist,
A cross of angels over me
From head to sole,
Tonight and until a year from tonight,
And tonight itself.

A Blessing on Everyone

As plentiful as the grass that grows,
Or the sand on the shore,
Or the dew on the lea,
So the blessings of the King of Grace
On every soul that was, that is, or will be.

The Emigrant's Prayer

Brigid that is in Faughart,
Blinne that is in Killeavey,
Bronagh that is in Ballinakill,
May you bring me back to Ireland.

(Title page illustration)